Copyright © 2019 by Nichelle Hodge

All rights reserved. No part of this publication may be reproduced, distributed, or transmitted in any form or by any means, including photocopying, recording, or other electronic or mechanical methods, without the prior written permission of the publisher, except in the case of brief quotations embodied in critical reviews and certain other noncommercial uses permitted by copyright law.

ISBN-13: 978-1-970079-52-4

Published and edited by:
Opportune Independent Publishing Co.
113 N. Live Oak Street
Houston, TX 77003
(832) 263-1700
www.opportunepublishing.com

This book is dedicated to the survivors, overcomers, and fellow victors. Yes, the abuse was real! It hurt and you have scars. Even your soul was wounded. Yet you've made it! You can boldly proclaim your liberty and courageously help set other captives free.

PAGE 14

ACKNOWLEDGEMENTS

I acknowledge my Heavenly Father, God. His only Son, My Savior, Jesus Christ. And my Life Coach, Comforter, Companion, and Helper, the Holy Spirit. It is because of my acceptance of, belief in, and acting upon the Word of God, that I am an Overcomer. All that I've had to endure has been for a purpose. Through the pain, I was made whole. Every tear that I've shed not gone without notice.

One of my all-time favorite promises that I remind God of often. This promise has been fulfilled many times over, and for that, I am eternally grateful.

I would also like to acknowledge my son, Jeremiah Hodge, who endured the growing pains of his mom. He is truly a God send. His temperament balances me much. To my sisters who've lived through some of the struggles too. Thank God that we don't look like what we've been through! To my friends who've provided wise counsel, been a listening ear, a shoulder to cry on, and even pieces of iron who help keep me accountable and sharp to continue on this journey. Many blessings for your faithfulness.

To all who have provided a covering spiritually along the way, please know that I believe in putting the Word to work. It's more than believing and shouting Amen. How will I apply what you've said to my life? Am I growing in my walk with Christ? Is there fruit in my life because of the seeds you planted? I have purposely set out to be better than who I was. Each day I get to work toward greatness. Even though I've stumbled along the way, I've gotten back up, and now with steady steps, I walk by faith. There is fruit in abundance. By your example, I can continue to sow seeds for Kingdom causes. Praise God! Hallelujah! AMEN

Table of Contents

Dedication	3
Acknowledgements	5
Introduction	11

Section I

1.	Letter of Forgiveness – Dear Abuser	25
2.	Child Abuse – Age 4	30
3.	Troubled Youth – Adolescent	36
4.	Rape – Age 15	44

Section II

5.	Blame, Guilt, Shame – Repercussions	56
6.	Human Trafficking – 20ish	67
7.	Mental Breakdown – 20ish	75
8.	Domestic Violence – 20ish	82
9.	Letter of Forgiveness – Dear Self	95
10.	No Longer a Victim	99

Bibliography	105
About the Author	109

INTRODUCTION

The experiences shared in this book are to enlighten you about the awareness of abuse and mental health. They are real factors that cause damage to the victim and the assailant. There are many signs. Your awareness, courage, and literacy can possibly help save a life. I hope that if you are in the midst of a crisis, know that you too can be free. Also, to those who know that abuse of any kind is taking place, please report it – see, say, do something!

Call 9-1-1

Domestic Violence Hotline
(800)799-7233
https://www.thehotline.org

Mental Health
(800)622-HELP (4357)
https://www.samhsa.gov/find-help/national-helpline

JOHN 16:33 TLB

Here on earth you will have many trials and sorrows; but cheer up, for I have overcome the world."

Mental Health is a subject that many families avoid talking about. Yet, we can identify at least one individual in our own families who has been plagued by such. We may be quick to label them, but aren't interested in getting to the root of the issue, or even being consistent with getting them the help that they so desperately need.

I recall hearing stories that my maternal grandmother suffered with mental illness. No one cared to explain what it meant, how it was dealt with, or is this something that will have an effect on the generations to come. When I personally suffered a mental breakdown in my early twenties, I admit the whole idea of getting help escaped me; but I was determined to have and live a better quality of life, for me and my son. I received the help that I need from that crisis, but would continue to struggle silently with fear or relapsing.

There were numerous challenges along the way and many things that I had to learn. In order to maintain a healthy mind, I encourage you to surround yourself with love and support, be attentive to what's going on the inside of you, educate yourself about your condition, and seek professional help, if that's what's needed to get you back to optimal health.

The state of one's mind can either build or break an individual. Their condition doesn't just affect them, but also those closest to them. I solemnly believe that a person can receive help and or treatment, and fully recover over time. In addition to prayer, support, and medication if needed, all of this can result in a better quality of life.

Though I've suffered from anxiety, mood, and eating disorders, I wanted to get better. So, I did what was necessary to get there.

Research shows that there a five major categories of mental illness:

- *Anxiety disorders*
- *Mood disorders*
- *Schizophrenia and psychotic disorders*
- *Dementia*
- *Eating disorders*

I encourage you to learn more and become an advocate to help save a life. MentalHealth.gov is great resource to start with. There is much information available that can be used for educational purposes and a place of solace in a time of crisis.

On the subject of abuse, having experienced much, I do believe that the root of it is caused by there is a mental disorder that has not been yet treated.

What a person believes in their mind will show in how they care for themselves and others, whether positively or negatively. My life has been spared many times, and as I share with you in the pages that follow, I sincerely hope and pray that you will be more attentive to others around you. There is always something greater going on than what we can really see.

Fear can silence a victim, preventing them from getting the help they so desperately need. You can be their voice! Insecurity can hold someone hostage, but you can be a place of trust and safety to help them. Anxiety can make it seem as though there is no relief in site. However, I am a witness that trouble won't last always, the sun will shine again, and there is joy on the other side of sorrow.

Psalm 69:5, 19 NKJV

O God, You know my foolishness;

And my sins are not hidden from You.

You know my reproach, my shame, and my

dishonor;

My adversaries are all before You.

PAGE 1 24

LETTER OF FORGIVENESS

Dear Abuser,

I had no idea that you were so afraid, angry, or that you suffered with pain yourself. It is said and true that, "hurt people, hurt people"… Because of your pain, your words, and your deeds, they have caused greater pain, leaving physical scars and emotional wounds that took a lifetime to heal.

Out of the pain that I endured, I too ended up hurting others…through bitterness, resentment, and rejection. I am sorry and I forgive you! While some may think that I have a right to hold this against you,

I disagree. Holding all of this in for so long was never healthy for me! I had to let it go!

I am no longer a prisoner of this pain. I am NO LONGER A VICTIM! I am a SURVIVOR, an OVERCOMER who shouts VICTORIOUSLY – I AM FREE! Grace has been extended to me to live free of the pain that I endured over the years, and mercy kept me daily from drowning beneath the weight of what I had to go through. God protected me from taking revenge. Vengeance is truly His. It is the Lord to judge and repay. It is my duty as His servant and precious child, to surrender by casting all of my cares upon him, to, forgive and to love. AMEN

Luke 6:28 AMP

"Bless and show kindness to those who curse you,

pray for those who mistreat you."

Child Abuse - Age 4

What can a toddler do that one would afflict a child severely to the point of leaving them scarred for the rest of their lives? I was there, but I still don't believe that the punishment should've gone that far.

It was an evening when I was up being mischievous. For some strange reason, I decided to decorate the bathroom with my mom's makeup. Oooohh, did I make a mess! There was no covering it up. The consequences were almost detrimental. In addition to the tongue lashing, the gas range was lit and I had to hold the backside of my hands up over the flames. That form of punishment was extreme.

Through pleading and tears, I literally had to pass through the fire. My hands swelled, filled with puss and pain. I wasn't taken to the hospital for care. I was kept at home from school so no questions would be asked, so the authorities wouldn't be involved. This one crucial act created much fear for me as a child. Not only was I extremely afraid of fire, I didn't know what else could be done to me if I disobeyed!

To this day, I refuse to get tattoos because of my scarred hands. When people look at my left hand, they inquire about what happened. The scarring on the right isn't as noticeable. I avoided getting into all the details. The blemishes on my skin are a part of my identity.

The abuse was real! As I got older, I would try my limits and receive due discipline, but never again to this degree.

Out of anger I rebelled, not wanting to be confined to any rules that seemed to suppress my free will. Whether it was at home or school, if I felt threatened by authority, I would speak up or act out. I didn't understand back then that there was a healthier way for me to express how I felt. I thought that if those who were to protect me could harm me, what could I do as a minor, an adolescent child do to defend themselves?

One night while waiting to get home from bible study, I remember laughing about the forms of punishment used growing up for all the trouble I'd get into. This public display was not humorous to my mother. I'd learn just how displeasing it was when I reached home. A lecture was giving and lashes were shared. I regretted uttering a word earlier that night. I paced back and forth down the hall, contemplating my next move. Finally, I opened the back door of our third floor apartment, practically jumping down several flights of stairs, running for miles as if my life depended on it. To me, it really did, and I just knew I couldn't go back.

FACT: When a child doesn't feel safe at home, they act out. In school and other places. Their negative behavior, most times is a cry for help, that shouldn't be ignored. Instead of labeling a child, try to see what's really going on. Most people will add to the verbal lashing of the child, but many will not take a step to find out the reason for the disruptive behavior.

Troubled Youth – Adolescent

Outside of the scarred hands, I believe I earned every other lick I received. Maybe the suffering I endured as a small child sparked a wildfire inside of me. If boundaries were set, I'd press my way to see what they were and how far I could go to pass them. When I was rebuked, instead of asking why, I'd set out to find out the reason on my own. That curiosity only led to more pain. Eventually, my heart became hardened.

I was a stubborn and rebellious child. Angry because of my plight. I tried to behave, but could seem to get things right. The discipline seemed to wear me out.

From getting in trouble at school to staying out past curfew, it's like I would provoke my mother to discipline me. She was certainly sure not to spare the rod at all. I sought attention, but didn't know there was a healthier way to go about receiving any.

For years I continued to cry out through negative behavior. After running away from home, being assigned a case worker, moving from detention centers and group homes, I eventually ended up in foster care. I was weary of running and being known as a trouble maker. My foster mother was strict too, but as long as we followed the rules, we were free to explore and make it back to the house on time. When we disobeyed, there'd be consequences to pay. I learned that it didn't take beating or threatening a child to get a point across.

I didn't trust easily, so I didn't keep too much company around me. I was much of an introverted loner. I also didn't think it was fair to accuse others for the trouble I got into. I thought that I if I was bad enough to do it, influenced or not, then it was my trouble to bear alone.

The lies that I started to believe was that the only way for me to receive love was to do what others wanted me to do, or act out for some attention, which was better than being ignored. I still lived in fear, but masked it behind a negative attitude. I wore a frown all the time and had a fist full of rage in my pocket, just in case. I was afraid of rejection too, but would be the first one to push others away so they didn't have to leave or abandon me.

It took a long time to find my voice and learn to speak truth from my soul. From what I learned, through the genuine care of others, not everyone was out to harm me…

PAGE / 41

ROMANS 7:15 NKJV

For what I am doing, I do not understand.

For what I will to do, that I do not practice; but

what I hate, that I do.

PAGE / 43

RAPE - AGE 15

The family court judge gave me six months to get my act together. If I could prove that I was mature enough, with less attitude and more respect, I'd be released back into my mother's care. I was finally making peace with my mom and now she's moving away. After twenty-five years of living in the United States, she decided it was time to return to her native land. She left the country for good the summer of 1992. I had to do something! I didn't want to be a ward of the state until I turned eighteen. How was I supposed to survive this!?! I did exactly what the judge instructed me to do. It took determination and self-control, but I was released from the state of Massachusetts, January 1993. I was now free to be reunited with my family.

I was an unaccompanied minor, with a one-way ticket, flying to my new home. After getting my bags, I went to the dock to board a ferry that would sail from St. Thomas. The weather and water mesmerized me. I sat still watching the ocean wave's crash beneath the large vessel. I safely reached my final destination.

Moving to Tortola, British Virgin Islands seemed like a fairy tale. My mom greeted me with a hug and we boarded the safari taxi from West End and drove to Purcell. It was all so surreal. The drive was refreshing and sobering. I had to remember that this was a new place and try not to get into any trouble.

That thought was short lived. Not even on the island a full week and I was late coming back home, getting grounded for a month. My first outing was a horse race. That wasn't even the fun part. It was the dancing afterwards that caused me to forget I had a curfew. A small place surrounded by water had much activity to keep one engaged and into unnecessary trouble.

School was already in session and I was told there was no room for me at the local high school. So once I got registered, I had to travel daily by ferry to another island, Virgin Gorda to attend the school there. At first, I would get seasick. The movement of the boat sailing on the water at a safe speed took some getting used to. With the exception of one accident, falling down the boat's engine shaft, but not to my death, I made it through the rest of the school year in one piece. That summer was exciting. Basketball games, pageants, carnival… It was like living in Paradise! Of course with the beauty, there were a few ashes. In essence, there was more fire that I would have to pass through.

Being the new girl on island had its challenges. I walked a lot. It was a way for me to be one with my thoughts. I was born and raised in the States, so of course, I had an accent, but so did everyone else on the island. I tried dating, but being in high school, it wasn't something that I wanted to think to seriously about. I didn't know who I could trust. Tortola was different. Not like any place that I've ever been. It really felt that I was a foreigner in a strange place. Maybe I was! Relocating and leaving the country didn't guarantee my safety. It taught me that abuse comes in different forms – deceit, manipulation.

Soon someone took notice of me. A well-known individual made it his business to express interest in me. However, I declined. I noticed him when I went out, but didn't desire that kind of attention. After much persuasion and persistence, I accepted his invitation to visit and hang out. We were not alone in the house. His friends were also over listening to music and having a good time. He pulled me to the side and let me know he wanted to be alone with me. I didn't feel threatened at the time.

As time progressed, he got closer. It made me uncomfortable. The music got louder, as if to drown out the sound of my voice that would soon escalate in screaming for help. He forced himself on me. Grabbing me. Pulling at my clothes. Held my hands and feet close to him as if I was an animal. I shouted helplessly, tried to break away, but he cornered me, locking me in. The louder I would cry out, the more laughter I would hear. I begged him to be set free. He laughed at me. He raped me, then threw me out. I ran for my life. I was in shock at what just took place. What was I to do!?! Who could I tell!?! Who would believe me!?!

I scrubbed myself in the shower to no avail, trying to wash away the filth that I felt. I hated myself. I blamed myself. "If I had continued to ignore him, this would have never happened!" "How could I let this happen?" "I told him to stop, to let me go, to leave me alone…" Why didn't he listen!?!" These questions played repeatedly in my mind.

This one heinous act added to the river of pain that I carried. My heart was filled with even more anger and I desperately wanted revenge, but I didn't retaliate against him. I let the anger poison me, expecting him to die. Another part of me died that day. I was numb and didn't know when or if it was possible to be restored.

Through a series of events, I returned to the States to finish high school. In spite of the physical scars and soulful wounds, there were positive attempts to make something better of my life...

ROMANS 8:1 NKJV

There is therefore now no condemnation to those

who are in Christ Jesus,

Who do not walk according to the flesh, but

according to the Spirit.

Blame, Guilt, Shame

– Repercussions

Here I was, a former ward of the state, still a minor who was left to pretty much fend for herself. The journey was rough, lonely, and strenuous, but by the grace of God, I graduated from South High Community School in June, 1995.

One would think that of all that I endured on the island of paradise, why would I want to return.

That decision was hard to make, but by being in familiar territory, you learn how to survive.

I planned on going to college once I graduated. I even got accepted to the University of the Virgin Islands in St. Thomas. Unfortunately, due to a lack of financial resources, that dream was deferred.

Since I was unable to go to college, it was time to look for work. I briefly worked at a local supermarket, but decided that wasn't what I wanted to do. I then got a job at an offshore trust company where I learned how to create and dissolve corporations. Shortly after, I'd be transferred upstairs to the accounting department. That move was the beginning of a promising career, but not without challenges.

I got pregnant at the age of nineteen and returned to the States to prepare for the arrival of my unborn child. I had a health pregnancy, physically. Emotionally and mentally, I was a wreck. I cried almost every day. Thinking about what I needed, but didn't have. I felt helpless. I didn't think of harming myself or my child, but I struggled with thoughts of survival. I slept on an air mattress for most of my pregnancy, and had morning sickness well into my third trimester. I tried to keep a smile on my face in public, but when I returned home, I'd fall into a state of depression. Tried to get involved with a local church, but during one service I attended, while going up to give an offering, someone managed to rob me. When I reported the incident to the police, they said it was unfortunate, but they received similar complaints from that location before.

Not only did I struggle with depression, I felt guilty for having a child young and out of wedlock. Growing up in the church, things that you learn can sometimes be taken out of context, leaving you in a state that is opposite than what the bible intended.

Six weeks after giving birth to my son, we left Georgia on a one-way flight and to move back to Tortola. My mother was very helpful with helping me raise my son, her first grandson. I am forever grateful for the bond that was created between them, the care that she showed, and the unconditional love that was given without a second thought.

I shared with my mother that I needed help with raising my son. I didn't have this baby alone, so I shouldn't have to be the only one responsible for him. I requested assistance from his biological father on multiple occasions and was denied. It was the rejection that made me involve the courts. That decision caused more pain for me, but it was something that I got used to living with. His father resented me for involving the courts to hold him accountable to help me to care for our son. Even after the court order, he wanted nothing to do with us because of me. I didn't have time to let the rejection hinder me, I had to see to it that my son was cared for.

After talking things over with my mom, she agreed to keep and help raise my son so I could return to the States to go to college. I believed that furthering my education would help to better our lives. I was excited because a dream that I had was now becoming a reality. While I couldn't attend school full-time, I was able to work during the day and go to class at night. That worked out temporarily. The living arrangements that I had were not working out. It became difficult for me to attend school and work at the same time. I made it through a few semesters, but didn't return due to having to work multiple jobs to support myself and my son who lived out of the country. The expenses and priceless commitments of having a child taught me to not be careless in relationships. I didn't have time to date. I was in hustle mode. Yeah, I kept a day job and worked overnight too. I was constantly thinking of how can I make money and not have to work so hard.

The answer to that question nearly cost my life…

Proverbs 14:12 NKJV

There is a way that seems right to a man,

But its end is the way of death.

Human Trafficking

20ish

In my twenties, there were some people, places, and things that I wish I never met, visited, or done! Yet, without the experiences, I would've probably not grown into the mature woman that I am today.

The proverb that bad company corrupts good character is sort of an understatement. Corruption can be subtle, but it can lead to devastation and destruction. I didn't know that my actions were a sign of being discontented. I lacked faith and thought I had to try to make things happen on my own. A prodigal daughter who was alone living a riotous living filled with pride couldn't see that trouble was lurking in the shadows.

A friend of a friend knew someone who had some light work that needed to be done. I volunteered without asking any questions. Had I known all the specifics I would have bailed. The rent had to be paid along with international childcare, utilities, and groceries. So here I was, caught up with a group of people who had access to money that I needed. Ignorance and stupidity near destroyed me.

I was sick when I got on the plane in the first place, headed to a strange place with some of that money. My job was to deliver the money in exchange for a package. What did it contain? That wasn't my business. Don't ask. Don't tell. Completely unknown to me, that I was being watched. I made it through the security checkpoint and was almost on the plane, when I was detained and held for questioning. I didn't say a word. Fear set in. Anger blurred my vision. Reality woke me up and the charges were filed. I was detained as a first offender. After serving several months, I was released. Much time has passed, but with undeserving grace, everlasting mercy, along with good legal counsel, the charges dropped as a result of being a victim entangled in a human trafficking scheme.

Trying to earn money fast cost time, relationships, and reputation. I wasn't completely devastated, but I hated how desperate I had become. I thought I had to do whatever I could to survive. After all of the hustle and bustle, there was only loss.

The struggle to survive began to take a greater toll on me. I drifted even further into depression, and starting isolating myself. Outside of work and occasionally church, I'd go to the market.

Soon my appetite began to fail. I quickly lost weight, cut off all my hair, and starting to lose my mind…

1 Samuel 16:15 AMP

Saul's servants said to him, "Behold, an evil spirit from God is tormenting you.

Mental Breakdown 2015

The days were long and the nights were lonely. Although I was making progress, I seemed to have fallen, and I didn't have a desire to carry on. I called my twin sister and told her to tell my mom and my son that I loved them. I went home and went to bed, not caring if I woke up. I did wake up and the days followed were a blur. I remember walking for miles as though I was lost, running into traffic, hoping a car would hit me, even tried hanging myself to no avail. The police were called and I was admitted into the hospital for a mental evaluation. I had completely lost it.

While I was in the hospital, I was sedated and given medication to keep me in a calm state. Each day I got up and went through the motions. I was quiet and kept to myself. There was a patient who would harass me constantly. This taunting frustrated me. Finally, I came to my senses. I boldly told the doctor that I was not crazy and it was time for me to go. After being evaluated again, I was released and allowed to return home. When I got home, I was greeted warmly by my mother and my growing son.

Life pressures overwhelmed me and I crashed hard. Yet, I believe that God saw to it that I knew it was only Him that delivered me. My mother was there through the process, but it was up to me to fight for the life that I wanted to love.

While my son was away, I hustled and worked hard to care for him. He was now living at home with me full time.

Once again I was afraid. "How am I supposed to raise a child on my own?" I watched my mom do it. Other single parents too, by themselves. As best as they could raising children, and even helping to raise their grandchildren too.

The plans that I had were no longer working. The dream was deferred again. The reality was that I had to find a better way to raise my son. Georgia became a place that only reminded me of more sorrow.

I packed up our belongings, and with a one-way ticket, we were on a Greyhound bus heading back to Worcester, MA. I knew that it was time to grow up and why not return to where life started for me. If I could survive Massachusetts, the Caribbean, maybe I'd gain some insight and strength, and with confidence someday I'd return to Georgia.

PSALM 37:23 NKJV

The steps of a good man are ordered by the

Lord,

And He delights in his way.

PAGE 1 81

Domestic Violence 20ish

Growing up in Worcester, MA had both good and not so pleasant memories. However, I knew that there was no room for me to mess things up. I came back to Massachusetts for specific reasons. To mature, to work, and to raise my son as best as possible. I was sure to return to Georgia when I had a solid plan in mind.

Out of all the tribulations that I've lived through, I'm glad that I made through. I had my son at twenty and I wanted to be there for him as long as

I could be. I had some support when raising him. My mom welcomed him to the Caribbean for summer vacations. I had a baby sitter and other help along the way. I could hang out with friends, travel, and create good memories as a young adult.

One night, a few friends and I drove out to Boston to hang out. We stayed out for hours, dancing. Life seemed to be turning around for me. My son was in school and the plan was coming together. Then I met a man. He was strong, handsome, and hurting. I didn't know it then, but as we got to know each other more, I became a sounding board to that pain.

Remember, hurt people hurt people. I was a little older, but still naïve. We became heavily involved and I began to care greatly for this man. He would tell me that he didn't like me spending so much time with my friends. The more I spent time with him, the less I had time for family and friends. He drew me in with his attentiveness and smooth speech, but I didn't know is was a sign for me to flee. I was in denial about some of things that I saw. I believed he loved me and my son. I refused to listen to anyone who told me differently. He would drink and smoke to numb himself from the physical pain that he felt. He also made sure that when I was with him I was isolated from having anyone near me.

In spite of the distance I traveled and disputes we'd have, I continued to stay with him. His family was getting used to seeing me there. If there weren't any activities planned at home, I'd get in my car and drive a little over an hour to Dorchester. It's like I had two homes with separate families.

On a bright summer day, we decided to take his children to the fair. We split up the group so everyone was looked after and could still have a good time. There was joy and laughter for most of the day.

I remember watching him and seeing a shift in his demeanor. I was concerned as to what had taken place, but didn't want to address the issue in front of the kids.

After being out in the hot sun for several hours, we went to the house to have dinner and settle in for the night. The kids were upstairs hanging out and we were left to ourselves. Being alone with him, I inquired about what took place that caused him to seem distant. He allowed his mind to wander to a frequent place that made him feel inadequate. He suffered from a work injury and seeing us out today, he wanted to do more. It frustrated him to not be able to provide for his family the way he so desired. I understood, but assured him that everyone had a good time. Still venting his frustration, instead of staying silent, I spoke up and said that he shouldn't feel bad about himself, nor should he drown his sorrows with alcohol or smoke. I had heard enough and I didn't feel like stroking his ego.

It is true that somethings are better left unsaid. What happened next, I wasn't prepared for. Like a roaring lion looking to devour his prey, he leaped toward me with much force that I didn't have time to react. He took both of his hands, wrapped them around my neck, and pinned me down to the cemented ground. His mother and brother could hear the commotion, but they didn't know that it escalated this far. When they did look outside and see me struggling for my life, they rushed to help. I could faintly hear his mother begging him to let me go, while his brother tried fighting him off me, but he wouldn't let go. His anger had blinded him and he was going to hold me there until I was lifeless. He finally released me, cursing at me, looking at me with such hatred instead of the love that I knew earlier that day. I gasped for air, through tears trying to catch my breath. I got into my car and drove away as fast as I could. If the truth that I spoke during a heated argument could cause a man that I loved to want to take my life, I needed to be far away as possible.

Words can provoke others toward negative actions. However, under no circumstance is it safe to stay in a relationship where you fear for your life. There was distance between us, but he had a set of keys to my home. I lived in gross fear months after the attack. Hearing commotion outside my door or seeing cars that were similar driving along the road, made me seek a new place of safety for me and my son.

I hated living in fear of another human being! It wasn't enough for me to change the locks or travel an alternate route back home. For my sanity and the safety of my son, moving was what I believed to be best.

We had a brand new start. With the move of courage and sincere apologies to my family and friends, I once again had the support that I needed. It was time to leave a toxic relationship and another very dark place in my life.

It storms from time to time, but when the rain stops and the winds cease, it's clear enough to see the bright sun.

PSALM 30:5 NKJV

For His anger is but for a moment,

His favor is for life;

Weeping may endure for a night,

But joy comes in the morning.

PAGE | 94

Letter of Forgiveness

This letter was initially written May 2013, and published March 28, 2016. I felt it necessary to share the contents of it with you.

"Dear Self,

I forgive you. For your imperfections and insecurities. For the times you were dishonest, unfaithful, and timid. For when you failed to listen to the advice and words of encouragement that you've given so many people. Most of all, for your weaknesses, while trying to appear strong... I forgive you. So, now I need you to do this for me. Accept it! Let go! And LIVE without any more regrets. I love you!"

2 Corinthians 2: 14 ERV

But thanks be to God, who always leads us in victory through Christ. God uses us to spread his knowledge everywhere like a sweet-smelling perfume.

No Longer a Victim

I found my voice and will shout from the mountain tops about the grace and mercy that was extended and shown to me throughout the years. God had spared my life, again, again, again, and again... Sharing these experiences with you all have not been to invoke sympathy, but to make you aware that a life that is filled with abuse, pain, fear, and sorrow, can be one that a person no longer wants to live.

Fortunately, I had an encounter with my Savior, Jesus Christ along the way and He's forgiven me, healed me, comforts me, redeemed me, and is restoring me daily. I know that I am loved and cared for. I also know not to be too hard on myself, and try best not to take things personally.

I am a vessel that was chosen to be used for His glory. The trials and tribulations are a part of my story. The pain was a part of my purpose.

I believe that those who abused me had their own pain and suffering to go through too. I've forgiven them so that I could be totally free, and share my story to help others be liberated. Being spiritually grounded helps me not to be consumed with negative thoughts. Christian counseling has also helped me to release things that were out of my control. As long as I have breath, I know that God is not through with me yet!

Sometimes ALL that we endure seems unbearable. I declare as a living witness, you can enjoy the gift of freedom, both physically and mentally. I no longer cry for what has been done. I can't change the past. I choose to not let it interfere with my present. Like my life, my future is in God's hands. Please do not ignore the signs! There are many and could be exhibited by anyone as a cry for help. Listen and head to their cry. Pray in faith, but act quickly. Thank you!

ROMANS 8:28 NKJV

And we know that all things work together

for good to those who love God, to those who are

the called according to His purpose.

PAGE / 104

BIBLIOGRAPHY

Hodge, N. (2016, April 18) It's Time to Talk About (It)!

https://www.linkedin.com/pulse/its-time-talk-nichelle-hodge/

Hodge, N. (2016, April 6) Are You In Good Company?

https://www.linkedin.com/pulse/you-good-company-nichelle-hodge/

1 Peter 5:10 AMP

After you have suffered for a little while, the God of all grace [who imparts His blessing and favor], who called you to His own eternal glory in Christ, will Himself complete, confirm, strengthen, and establish you [making you what you ought to be]

About the Author

Nichelle A. Hodge is a management consultant who focuses on accounting and payroll. She possesses a Bachelor's degree in Accounting and a Master's degree in Management and Leadership. She has written many articles throughout the years that have been published on LinkedIn. She owns both a consulting and craft business. NAH II Enterprises, LLC specializes in accounting and management services. Fruit Blankets creates hand crafted customized baby blankets. Nichelle is a daughter, mother, sister, and friend. Also an author, artist, educator, and consultant. She enjoys cooking, reading, writing, traveling, and $5 Movie Tuesdays at most AMC or New Vision Theatres. She is a life-long learner that is committed to a life of service. She is available for speaking engagements and to facilitate small group classes that encourage the growth of women in the Kingdom, body of Christ.

NAH II Enterprises, LLC
P.O. Box 1643
Stone Mountain, GA 30086
nahiienterprisesllc@gmail.com

www.ingramcontent.com/pod-product-compliance
Lightning Source LLC
Chambersburg PA
CBHW071903070526
44583CB00016B/1819